egg beaters®

Healthy Real Egg Product

Delicious Recipes for Healthy Living

PUBLICATIONS INTERNATIONAL, LTD.

This edition published by Publications International, Ltd.,
7373 N. Cicero Ave., Lincolnwood, IL 60646.

Photography: Sacco Productions Limited, Chicago

Pictured on the front cover *(clockwise from top right):* Zucchini Mushroom Frittata *(page 10),* Mocha Marbled Cheesecake *(page 90),* Penne Primavera *(page 62)* and Honey-Dijon Salad with Shrimp *(page 42).*

Pictured on the back cover *(top to bottom):* Silver Dollar Pancakes with Mixed Berry Topping *(page 14),* Stuffed Shells Florentine *(page 58),* Fruit Tart *(page 74)* and Breakfast Burritos with Tomato-Basil Topping *(page 8).*

ISBN: 0-7853-1739-2

Manufactured in U.S.A.

8   7   6   5   4   3   2   1

Nutritional Analysis: Every recipe in this cookbook is followed by a nutritional analysis that lists certain nutrient values for a single serving. The analysis of each recipe includes all the ingredients that are listed in that recipe, *except* ingredients listed as "optional" or "for garnish." If a range is offered for an ingredient ("$1/8$ to $1/4$ teaspoon" for example), the *first* amount given was used to calculate the nutrition information. If an ingredient is presented with an option ("$1/2$ cup blueberries or raspberries" for example), the *first* item listed was used to calculate the nutrition information. Foods shown in photographs on the same serving plate and offered as "serve with" or "garnish with" suggestions at the end of the recipe are *not* included in the nutritional analysis. Every effort has been made to give accurate nutritional data. However, because numerous variables account for a wide range of values for certain foods, all nutrient values that appear in this publication should be considered approximate.

egg beaters

Healthy Real Egg Product

Delicious Recipes for Healthy Living

We're Good Eggs

Eggs have always been considered one of nature's most nutritious foods—a good source of protein, vitamins and minerals. But the experts have now labeled eggs forbidden because of the fat and cholesterol content found in the yolk. There is a way, though, to still enjoy eggs and all your favorite egg recipes—just replace the eggs with Egg Beaters. Egg Beaters Healthy Real Egg Product is made from 99% real egg whites with added vitamins and minerals and no preservatives. Egg Beaters is naturally fat-free, contain zero cholesterol and is a good source of protein.

Egg yolks contain five grams of fat per yolk and are high in cholesterol (213 mg per yolk). Egg Beaters has as much protein as a whole egg, but with no fat, no cholesterol and 40% fewer calories because they are 99% real egg whites, with no yolk.

Egg Beaters can be used just as you would use whole eggs, as a main dish or as an ingredient in a recipe. Simply substitute ¼ cup Egg Beaters (two ounces) for each whole egg. For recipes calling for up to two egg yolks, use three tablespoons Egg Beaters per yolk. Egg Beaters also is a pasteurized egg product, so it is safe to use in recipes calling for whole uncooked eggs, such as Caesar salad dressing, béarnaise and hollandaise sauce, egg nog and breakfast protein shakes.

EGG BEATERS OUTPERFORMS SHELL EGGS:		
	EGG BEATERS (¼ cup)	**One Whole** **Shell Egg** (¼ cup)
Fat (g)	0	5
Cholesterol (mg)	0	213
Calories	30	75
Protein (g)	6	6
Carbohydrates (g)	1	1

HELPFUL HINTS

Skillet Scrambling: Pour Egg Beaters into a nonstick skillet over medium heat. Let product set for 30 seconds. Push cooked portion to center with a spatula. Do not stir.

Microwave Scrambling: Pour ½ cup Egg Beaters into a microwavable bowl. Cover and cook at HIGH (100%) power for 1 minute. Stir. Cook ½ to 1 minute more until set but slightly moist.

Hard-Cooked: Pour Egg Beaters into a nonstick skillet. Cover; cook for 10 minutes over very low heat. Cool, then chop into cubes and use to make egg salad or egg sandwiches.

Breading: Use Egg Beaters to coat chicken, fish or other foods before cooking with bread crumbs or flour.

SOME FINAL INFORMATION

Egg Beaters can be found in both the refrigerator case and in the frozen food section of your supermarket. Refrigerated Egg Beaters is ready to pour straight from the package. It will keep in the refrigerator until the expiration date printed on the package, or up to seven days once opened. Frozen Egg Beaters is easy to defrost, and can be stored in the freezer for up to one year. Once defrosted, it can be refrigerated for up to seven days. Do not refreeze.

EGG BEATERS ADVANTAGE

- More Convenient than Shell Eggs
- No Fat, No Cholesterol
- Made from Real Eggs
- Great Source of Protein
- Added Vitamins and Minerals
- Pasteurized for Safety/Can use Uncooked
- No Preservatives
- Resealable, Easy-to-use Packaging

1/4 CUP = 1 EGG

Homestyle Breakfasts

BREAKFAST BURRITOS WITH TOMATO–BASIL TOPPING

Prep Time: 15 minutes   **Cook Time: 25 minutes**

1 large tomato, diced
2 teaspoons finely chopped basil
    (*or* ½ teaspoon dried basil
    leaves)
1 medium potato, peeled and
    shredded (about 1 cup)
¼ cup chopped onion

2 teaspoons Fleischmann's
    Margarine
1 cup EGG BEATERS
⅛ teaspoon ground black pepper
4 (8-inch) flour tortillas, warmed
⅓ cup shredded reduced-fat
    Cheddar cheese

In small bowl, combine tomato and basil; set aside.

In large nonstick skillet, over medium heat, sauté potato and onion in margarine until tender. Pour Egg Beaters into skillet; sprinkle with pepper. Cook, stirring occasionally until mixture is set.

Divide egg mixture evenly between tortillas; top with cheese. Fold tortillas over egg mixture. Top with tomato mixture.   *Makes 4 servings*

Nutrition information per serving:

Calories	226	Total Fat	6 g	Sodium	364 mg
Cholesterol	5 mg	Saturated Fat	1 g	Dietary Fiber	2 g

Breakfast Burritos with Tomato-Basil Topping

ZUCCHINI MUSHROOM FRITTATA

Prep Time: 20 minutes   Cook Time: 20 minutes

1½ cups EGG BEATERS
½ cup (2 ounces) shredded
    reduced-fat Swiss cheese
¼ cup skim milk
½ teaspoon garlic powder
¼ teaspoon seasoned pepper
    Nonstick cooking spray

1 medium zucchini, shredded
    (1 cup)
1 medium tomato, chopped
1 (4-ounce) can sliced
    mushrooms, drained
    Tomato slices and fresh basil
    leaves, for garnish

In medium bowl, combine Egg Beaters, cheese, milk, garlic powder and seasoned pepper; set aside.

Spray 10-inch ovenproof nonstick skillet lightly with nonstick cooking spray. Over medium-high heat, sauté zucchini, tomato and mushrooms in skillet until tender. Pour egg mixture into skillet, stirring well. Cover; cook over low heat for 15 minutes or until cooked on bottom and almost set on top. Remove lid and place skillet under broiler for 2 to 3 minutes or until desired doneness. Slide onto serving platter; cut into wedges to serve. Garnish with tomato slices and basil. *Makes 6 servings*

Nutrition information per serving:

Calories	71	Total Fat	2 g	Sodium	147 mg
Cholesterol	7 mg	Saturated Fat	1 g	Dietary Fiber	0 g

CHOCOLATE BREAKFAST SHAKE

Prep Time: 5 minutes

3 cups EGG BEATERS
½ cup chocolate-flavored syrup

⅓ cup nonfat dry milk
2 teaspoons wheat germ

In electric blender container, blend Egg Beaters, chocolate syrup, dry milk and wheat germ until well combined. Serve immediately.

Makes 4 (8-ounce) servings

Nutrition information per serving:

Calories	184	Total Fat	0 g	Sodium	314 mg
Cholesterol	1 mg	Saturated Fat	0 g	Dietary Fiber	0 g

Zucchini Mushroom Frittata

MUSHROOM–HERB OMELET

Prep Time: 10 minutes   Cook Time: 20 minutes

1 cup EGG BEATERS
1 tablespoon chopped fresh
    parsley
1 teaspoon finely chopped fresh
    oregano, basil or thyme
    (*or* ¼ teaspoon dried)

2 cups sliced fresh mushrooms
2 teaspoons Fleischmann's
    Margarine, divided

In small bowl, combine Egg Beaters, parsley and oregano, basil or thyme; set aside.

In 8-inch nonstick skillet, over medium heat, sauté mushrooms in 1 teaspoon margarine until tender; set aside. In same skillet, over medium heat, melt ½ teaspoon margarine. Pour half the egg mixture into skillet. Cook, lifting edges to allow uncooked portion to flow underneath. When almost set, spoon half of mushrooms over half of omelet. Fold other half over mushrooms; slide onto serving plate. Repeat with remaining margarine, egg mixture and mushrooms.   *Makes 2 servings*

Nutrition information per serving:

Calories	112	Total Fat	4 g	Sodium	239 mg
Cholesterol	0 mg	Saturated Fat	1 g	Dietary Fiber	1 g

POTATO & ONION FRITTATA

Prep Time: 5 minutes   Cook Time: 15 minutes

1 small baking potato, peeled,
    halved and sliced ⅛-inch
    thick (about ½ cup)
¼ cup chopped onion
1 clove garlic, minced

Dash ground black pepper
1 tablespoon Fleischmann's
    Margarine
1 cup EGG BEATERS

In 8-inch nonstick skillet, over medium-high heat, sauté potato, onion, garlic and pepper in margarine until tender. Pour Egg Beaters evenly into skillet over potato mixture. Cook without stirring for 5 to 6 minutes or until cooked on bottom and almost set on top. Carefully turn frittata; cook for 1 to 2 minutes more or until done. Slide onto serving platter; cut into wedges to serve.   *Makes 2 servings*

Nutrition information per serving:

Calories	174	Total Fat	6 g	Sodium	204 mg
Cholesterol	0 mg	Saturated Fat	1 g	Dietary Fiber	0 g

APPLE RAISIN PANCAKES

Prep Time: 10 minutes   Cook Time: 15 minutes

2 cups all-purpose flour
2 tablespoons sugar
1 tablespoon baking powder
2 teaspoons ground cinnamon
1¾ cups skim milk

⅔ cup EGG BEATERS
5 tablespoons Fleischmann's
    Margarine, melted, divided
¾ cup chopped apple
¾ cup seedless raisins

In large bowl, combine flour, sugar, baking powder and cinnamon. In medium bowl, combine milk, Egg Beaters and 4 tablespoons margarine; stir into dry ingredients just until blended. Stir in apple and raisins.

Brush large nonstick griddle or skillet with some of remaining margarine; heat over medium-high heat. Using ¼ cup batter for each pancake, pour batter onto griddle. Cook until bubbly; turn and cook until lightly browned. Repeat with remaining batter using remaining margarine as needed to make 16 pancakes. *Makes 16 (4-inch) pancakes*

Nutrition information per pancake:

Calories	134	Total Fat	4 g	Sodium	157 mg
Cholesterol	1 mg	Saturated Fat	1 g	Dietary Fiber	1 g

ITALIAN OMELET

Prep Time: 10 minutes   Cook Time: 10 minutes

¼ cup chopped tomato
¼ cup (1 ounce) shredded part-
    skim mozzarella cheese
¼ teaspoon dried basil leaves
¼ teaspoon dried oregano leaves

1 teaspoon Fleischmann's
    Margarine
1 cup EGG BEATERS
Chopped fresh parsley, for
    garnish

In small bowl, combine tomato, cheese, basil and oregano; set aside.

In 8-inch nonstick skillet, over medium heat, melt margarine. Pour Egg Beaters into skillet. Cook, lifting edges to allow uncooked portion to flow underneath. When almost set, spoon tomato mixture over half of omelet. Fold other half over tomato mixture; cover and continue to cook for 1 to 2 minutes. Slide onto serving plate. Garnish with parsley.

Makes 2 servings

Nutrition information per serving:

Calories	119	Total Fat	4 g	Sodium	286 mg
Cholesterol	8 mg	Saturated Fat	2 g	Dietary Fiber	0 g

SILVER DOLLAR PANCAKES WITH MIXED BERRY TOPPING

Prep Time: 20 minutes   Cook Time: 20 minutes

1¼ cups all-purpose flour
2 tablespoons sugar
2 teaspoons baking soda
1½ cups buttermilk
½ cup EGG BEATERS

3 tablespoons Fleischmann's
  Margarine, melted, divided
Mixed Berry Topping (recipe
  follows)

In large bowl, combine flour, sugar and baking soda. Stir in buttermilk, Egg Beaters and 2 tablespoons margarine just until blended.

Brush large nonstick griddle or skillet with some of remaining margarine; heat over medium-high heat. Using 1 heaping tablespoon batter for each pancake, spoon batter onto griddle. Cook until bubbly; turn and cook until lightly browned. Repeat with remaining batter using remaining margarine as needed to make 28 pancakes. Serve hot with Mixed Berry Topping.

Makes 28 (2-inch) pancakes

MIXED BERRY TOPPING: In medium saucepan, over medium-low heat, combine 1 (12-ounce) package frozen mixed berries,* thawed, ¼ cup honey and ½ teaspoon grated gingerroot (*or* ⅛ teaspoon ground ginger). Cook and stir just until hot and well blended. Serve over pancakes.

*3 cups mixed fresh berries may be substituted.

Nutrition information per serving:

(4 pancakes, ¼ cup topping)

Calories	228		Total Fat	6 g		Sodium	491 mg
Cholesterol	2 mg		Saturated Fat	1 g		Dietary Fiber	1 g

Silver Dollar Pancakes with Mixed Berry Topping

CHILE SCRAMBLE

Prep Time: 5 minutes	Cook Time: 10 minutes

2 tablespoons minced onion
1 teaspoon Fleischmann's
   Margarine
1 cup EGG BEATERS

1 (4-ounce) can diced green
   chiles, drained
¼ cup whole kernel corn
2 tablespoons diced pimientos

In 10-inch nonstick skillet, over medium-high heat, sauté onion in margarine for 2 to 3 minutes or until onion is translucent. Pour Egg Beaters into skillet; cook, stirring occasionally until mixture is set. Stir in chiles, corn and pimientos; cook 1 minute more or until heated through.

Makes 2 servings

Nutrition information per serving:

Calories	118	Total Fat	2 g	Sodium	254 mg
Cholesterol	0 mg	Saturated Fat	0 g	Dietary Fiber	1 g

FRENCH TOAST STICKS

Prep Time: 15 minutes	Cook Time: 18 minutes

1 cup EGG BEATERS
⅓ cup skim milk
1 teaspoon ground cinnamon
1 teaspoon vanilla extract
2 tablespoons Fleischmann's
   Margarine, divided

16 (4×1×1-inch) sticks day-old
   white bread
Powdered sugar, optional
Maple-flavored syrup, optional

In shallow bowl, combine Egg Beaters, milk, cinnamon and vanilla.

In large nonstick griddle or skillet, over medium-high heat, melt 2 teaspoons margarine. Dip bread sticks in egg mixture to coat; transfer to griddle. Cook sticks on each side until golden, adding remaining margarine as needed. Dust lightly with powdered sugar and serve with syrup if desired.

Makes 4 servings

Nutrition information per serving:

(without powdered sugar or syrup)

Calories	217	Total Fat	7 g	Sodium	382 mg
Cholesterol	2 mg	Saturated Fat	1 g	Dietary Fiber	0 g

Chile Scramble

SWEET POTATO PANCAKES

Prep Time: 15 minutes   Cook Time: 20 minutes

¼ cup all-purpose flour
½ teaspoon dried rosemary
    leaves, crushed
⅛ to ¼ teaspoon ground black
    pepper
2 small sweet potatoes, peeled
    and shredded (about 3 cups)

1 cup EGG BEATERS
⅓ cup chopped onion
1 tablespoon Fleischmann's
    Margarine, divided
    Fat-free sour cream or yogurt,
    optional

In small bowl, combine flour, rosemary and pepper; set aside.

Pat shredded potatoes dry with paper towels. In medium bowl, combine potatoes, Egg Beaters and onion; stir in flour mixture. In large nonstick skillet, over medium-low heat, melt 2 teaspoons margarine. For each pancake, spoon about ⅓ cup potato mixture into skillet, spreading into a 4-inch circle. Cook for 5 minutes on each side or until golden; remove and keep warm. Repeat with remaining mixture, using remaining margarine as needed to make 8 pancakes. Serve hot with sour cream or yogurt if desired.

Makes 8 pancakes

Nutrition information per pancake:

(without sour cream)

Calories	127	Total Fat	2 g	Sodium	74 mg
Cholesterol	0 mg	Saturated Fat	0 g	Dietary Fiber	3 g

BLINTZES WITH RASPBERRY SAUCE

Prep Time: 30 minutes   Cook Time: 45 minutes

1 (16-ounce) container low fat
    cottage cheese (1% milkfat)
3 tablespoons EGG BEATERS
½ teaspoon sugar

10 prepared French Breakfast
    Crêpes (page 26)
    Raspberry Sauce (page 19)

In small bowl, combine cottage cheese, Egg Beaters and sugar; spread 2 tablespoonfuls mixture down center of each crêpe. Fold two opposite ends of each crêpe over filling, then fold in sides like an envelope. In lightly greased large nonstick skillet, over medium heat, place blintzes seam-side down. Cook for 4 minutes on each side or until golden brown. Serve hot with Raspberry Sauce.   *Makes 10 servings*

RASPBERRY SAUCE: In electric blender container or food processor, purée 1 (16-ounce) package frozen raspberries, thawed; strain. Stir in 2 tablespoons sugar. Serve over blintzes.

Nutrition information per serving:					
Calories	161	Total Fat	2 g	Sodium	231 mg
Cholesterol	2 mg	Saturated Fat	1 g	Dietary Fiber	0 g

CINNAMON FRENCH TOAST

Prep Time: 25 minutes   Cook Time: 15 minutes

1 cup EGG BEATERS
⅓ cup skim milk
1 teaspoon ground cinnamon
1 teaspoon vanilla extract
10 (1-inch-thick) slices French bread

2 tablespoons Fleischmann's Margarine, divided
Additional Fleischmann's Margarine, optional
Maple-flavored syrup, optional

In small bowl, combine Egg Beaters, milk, cinnamon and vanilla. Pour half of egg mixture into 13×9×2-inch baking pan. Arrange bread slices in pan; pour remaining egg mixture evenly over bread slices. Let stand for 15 to 20 minutes to absorb egg mixture.

In large nonstick griddle or skillet, over medium heat, melt 1 tablespoon margarine. Cook half the bread slices for 3 minutes on each side or until golden. Cook remaining bread slices using remaining 1 tablespoon margarine as needed. Serve topped with additional margarine and syrup if desired.   *Makes 5 servings*

Nutrition information per serving:					
(without additional margarine or syrup)					
Calories	260	Total Fat	7 g	Sodium	537 mg
Cholesterol	0 mg	Saturated Fat	1 g	Dietary Fiber	2 g

POTATO LATKES

Prep Time: 20 minutes   Cook Time: 18 minutes

⅔ cup EGG BEATERS
⅓ cup all-purpose flour
¼ cup grated onion
¼ teaspoon ground black pepper
4 large potatoes, peeled and
    shredded (about 4 cups)

3 tablespoons Fleischmann's
    Margarine, divided
1½ cups sweetened applesauce
Fresh chives, for garnish

In large bowl, combine Egg Beaters, flour, onion and pepper; set aside.

Pat shredded potatoes dry with paper towels. Stir into egg mixture. In large nonstick skillet, over medium-high heat, melt 1½ tablespoons margarine. For each pancake, spoon about ⅓ cup potato mixture into skillet, spreading into a 4-inch circle. Cook for 3 minutes on each side or until golden; remove and keep warm. Repeat with remaining mixture, using remaining margarine as needed to make 12 pancakes. Serve hot with applesauce. Garnish with chives.   *Makes 4 servings*

Nutrition information per serving:

Calories	460	Total Fat	12 g	Sodium	208 mg
Cholesterol	0 mg	Saturated Fat	4 g	Dietary Fiber	4 g

CHICKEN BROCCOLI FRITTATA

Prep Time: 15 minutes   Cook Time: 11 minutes

1 cup chopped fresh broccoli
    flowerettes
½ cup chopped cooked chicken
¼ cup chopped tomato
¼ cup chopped onion

¼ teaspoon dried tarragon leaves
1 tablespoon Fleischmann's
    Margarine
1 cup EGG BEATERS

In 10-inch nonstick skillet, over medium heat, sauté broccoli, chicken, tomato, onion and tarragon in margarine until tender-crisp. Reduce heat to low. Pour Egg Beaters evenly into skillet over chicken mixture. Cover; cook for 5 to 7 minutes or until cooked on bottom and almost set on top. Slide onto serving platter; cut into wedges to serve.   *Makes 2 servings*

Nutrition information per serving:

Calories	210	Total Fat	8 g	Sodium	301 mg
Cholesterol	31 mg	Saturated Fat	2 g	Dietary Fiber	3 g

Potato Latkes

WESTERN OMELET

Prep Time: 15 minutes   Cook Time: 10 minutes

½ cup finely chopped red or
  green bell pepper
⅓ cup cubed cooked potato
2 slices turkey bacon, diced
¼ teaspoon dried oregano leaves

2 teaspoons Fleischmann's
  Margarine, divided
1 cup EGG BEATERS
Fresh oregano sprig, for
  garnish

In 8-inch nonstick skillet, over medium heat, sauté bell pepper, potato, turkey bacon and dried oregano in 1 teaspoon margarine until tender.* Remove from skillet; keep warm.

In same skillet, over medium heat, melt remaining margarine. Pour Egg Beaters into skillet. Cook, lifting edges to allow uncooked portion to flow underneath. When almost set, spoon vegetable mixture over half of omelet. Fold other half over vegetable mixture; slide onto serving plate. Garnish with fresh oregano.   *Makes 2 servings*

*For frittata, sauté vegetables, turkey bacon and dried oregano in 2 teaspoons margarine. Pour Egg Beaters evenly into skillet over vegetable mixture. Cook without stirring for 4 to 5 minutes or until cooked on bottom and almost set on top. Carefully turn frittata; cook for 1 to 2 minutes more or until done. Slide onto serving platter; cut into wedges to serve.

Nutrition information per serving:					
Calories	147	Total Fat	6 g	Sodium	384 mg
Cholesterol	10 mg	Saturated Fat	1 g	Dietary Fiber	1 g

Western Omelet

PRALINE FRENCH TOAST

Prep Time: 30 minutes   Cook Time: 30 minutes

FRENCH TOAST

1 cup EGG BEATERS
⅓ cup skim milk
1 teaspoon ground cinnamon
1 teaspoon vanilla extract
2 tablespoons Fleischmann's
    Margarine, divided
10 slices white bread, divided

PRALINE SAUCE

½ cup pecan pieces
2 tablespoons Fleischmann's
    Margarine
½ cup firmly packed light brown
    sugar
½ cup maple-flavored syrup
⅓ cup seedless raisins

To prepare French Toast: In shallow bowl, combine Egg Beaters, milk, cinnamon and vanilla. In large nonstick griddle or skillet, over medium heat, melt 2 teaspoons margarine. Dip half the bread slices in egg mixture to coat; transfer to griddle. Cook 2 minutes on each side or until golden. Dip remaining bread slices in egg mixture to coat. Cook using remaining margarine as needed. Keep warm.

To prepare Praline Sauce: In 2-quart saucepan, over medium-low heat, sauté pecans in margarine until golden. Stir in brown sugar, syrup and raisins; heat until sugar dissolves, about 5 minutes. Serve warm over French Toast.

Makes 10 servings

Nutrition information per serving:
(1 slice, 2 tablespoons sauce)

Calories	251	Total Fat	9 g	Sodium	205 mg
Cholesterol	1 mg	Saturated Fat	1 g	Dietary Fiber	1 g

WHOLE WHEAT GRIDDLE CAKES WITH FRESH STRAWBERRY TOPPING

Prep Time: 20 minutes   Cook Time: 20 minutes

1¼ cups whole wheat flour
1¼ cups all-purpose flour
2 tablespoons sugar
1 tablespoon baking powder
1¾ cups skim milk

1 cup EGG BEATERS
3 tablespoons Fleischmann's
    Margarine, melted, divided
Fresh Strawberry Topping
(page 25)

In large bowl, combine flours, sugar and baking powder. Stir in milk, Egg Beaters and 2 tablespoons margarine just until blended. (Batter will be slightly lumpy.)

Brush large nonstick griddle or skillet with some of remaining margarine; heat over medium-high heat. Using ¼ cup batter for each pancake, pour batter onto griddle. Cook until bubbly; turn and cook until lightly browned. Repeat with remaining batter using remaining margarine as needed to make 16 pancakes. Serve hot with Fresh Strawberry Topping.

Makes 16 (5-inch) pancakes

FRESH STRAWBERRY TOPPING: In large bowl, combine 1 quart strawberries, sliced, and ¼ cup honey. Serve over pancakes.

Nutrition information per serving:

(1 pancake, 2½ tablespoons topping)

Calories	138	Total Fat	3 g	Sodium	113 mg
Cholesterol	1 mg	Saturated Fat	0 g	Dietary Fiber	2 g

BREAKFAST BREAD PUDDING WITH BERRY SAUCE

Prep Time: 15 minutes   Cook Time: 45 minutes

8 slices cinnamon raisin bread, cubed
2 cups skim milk
1 cup EGG BEATERS
¼ cup sugar
1 teaspoon vanilla extract
½ teaspoon ground nutmeg

½ cup maple-flavored syrup
2 tablespoons Fleischmann's Margarine
1 cup sliced strawberries
½ cup blueberries
1 teaspoon lemon juice
1 teaspoon lemon peel

Evenly divide bread cubes between 8 greased heatproof (6-ounce) custard cups or ramekins. In medium bowl, combine milk, Egg Beaters, sugar, vanilla and nutmeg. Evenly pour mixture over bread cubes. Place cups in roasting pan filled with 1-inch depth hot water. Bake at 325°F for 35 to 45 minutes or until set. Let stand for 5 minutes.

In small saucepan, heat syrup and margarine until blended. Stir in fruit, lemon juice and peel; heat through. Unmold puddings onto individual serving plates; serve with berry sauce.

Makes 8 servings

Nutrition information per serving:

Calories	214	Total Fat	4 g	Sodium	191 mg
Cholesterol	2 mg	Saturated Fat	1 g	Dietary Fiber	1 g

FRENCH BREAKFAST CRÊPES

Prep Time: 10 minutes   Cook Time: 40 minutes

1 cup all-purpose flour
1 cup skim milk
⅔ cup EGG BEATERS

1 tablespoon Fleischmann's
Margarine, melted

In medium bowl, combine flour, milk, Egg Beaters and margarine; let stand 30 minutes.

Heat lightly greased 8-inch nonstick skillet or crêpe pan over medium-high heat. Pour in scant ¼ cup batter, tilting pan to cover bottom. Cook for 1 to 2 minutes; turn and cook for 30 seconds to 1 minute more. Place on waxed paper. Stir batter and repeat to make 10 crêpes. Fill with desired fillngs or use in recipes calling for prepared crêpes.   *Makes 10 crêpes*

Nutrition information per crêpe:					
Calories	73	Total Fat	1 g	Sodium	51 mg
Cholesterol	0 mg	Saturated Fat	0 g	Dietary Fiber	0 g

STRAWBERRY YOGURT CRÊPES: In medium bowl, combine 1 pint low fat vanilla yogurt and 2 tablespoons orange-flavored liqueur or orange juice; reserve ½ cup. Stir 2 cups sliced strawberries into remaining yogurt mixture. Spoon ¼ cup strawberry mixture down center of each prepared crêpe; roll up. Top with reserved yogurt mixture.

Nutrition information per crêpe:					
Calories	129	Total Fat	2 g	Sodium	82 mg
Cholesterol	3 mg	Saturated Fat	1 g	Dietary Fiber	0 g

BLUEBERRY CRÊPES: In medium saucepan, combine 2 cups fresh or frozen blueberries, ⅓ cup water, 2 teaspoons lemon juice and 2 teaspoons cornstarch. Cook over medium-high heat, stirring frequently until mixture thickens and begins to boil. Reduce heat; simmer 1 minute. Chill. Spoon 2 tablespoons low fat vanilla yogurt down center of each prepared crêpe; roll up. Top with blueberry sauce.

Nutrition information per crêpe:					
Calories	120	Total Fat	2 g	Sodium	58 mg
Cholesterol	1 mg	Saturated Fat	0 g	Dietary Fiber	0 g

Strawberry Yogurt Crêpe

PB & J FRENCH TOAST

Prep Time: 25 minutes   Cook Time: 10 minutes

¼ cup blueberry preserves, or
  any flavor
6 slices whole wheat bread,
  divided
¼ cup creamy peanut butter
½ cup EGG BEATERS
¼ cup skim milk
2 tablespoons Fleischmann's
  Margarine

1 large banana, sliced
1 tablespoon honey
1 tablespoon orange juice
1 tablespoon dry roasted
  unsalted peanuts, chopped
Low fat vanilla yogurt,
  optional

Spread preserves evenly over 3 bread slices. Spread peanut butter evenly over remaining bread slices. Press preserves and peanut butter slices together to form 3 sandwiches; cut each diagonally in half. In shallow bowl, combine Egg Beaters and milk. In large nonstick griddle or skillet, over medium-high heat, melt margarine. Dip each sandwich in egg mixture to coat; transfer to griddle. Cook sandwiches for 2 minutes on each side or until golden. Keep warm.

In small bowl, combine banana slices, honey, orange juice and peanuts. Arrange sandwiches on platter; top with banana mixture. Serve warm with a dollop of yogurt if desired.   *Makes 6 servings*

Nutrition information per serving:

(without yogurt)

Calories	242	Total Fat	11 g	Sodium	262 mg
Cholesterol	1 mg	Saturated Fat	2 g	Dietary Fiber	3 g

PB & J French Toast

TRIPLE–DECKER VEGETABLE OMELET

Prep Time: 20 minutes   Cook Time: 30 minutes

1 cup finely chopped broccoli
½ cup diced red bell pepper
½ cup shredded carrot
⅓ cup sliced green onions
1 clove garlic, minced
2½ teaspoons Fleischmann's
    Margarine, divided
¾ cup low fat cottage cheese
    (1% milkfat), divided

1 tablespoon plain dry bread
    crumbs
1 tablespoon grated Parmesan
    cheese
½ teaspoon Italian seasoning
1½ cups EGG BEATERS, divided
⅓ cup chopped tomato
    Chopped fresh parsley, for
    garnish

In 8-inch nonstick skillet, over medium-high heat, sauté broccoli, bell pepper, carrot, green onions and garlic in 1 teaspoon margarine until tender. Remove from skillet; stir in ½ cup cottage cheese. Keep warm. Combine bread crumbs, Parmesan cheese and Italian seasoning; set aside.

In same skillet, over medium heat, melt ½ teaspoon margarine. Pour ½ cup Egg Beaters into skillet. Cook, lifting edges to allow uncooked portion to flow underneath. When almost set, slide unfolded omelet onto ovenproof serving platter. Top with half each of the vegetable mixture and bread crumb mixture; set aside.

Prepare 2 more omelets with remaining Egg Beaters and margarine. Layer 1 omelet onto serving platter over vegetable and bread crumb mixture; top with remaining vegetable mixture and bread crumb mixture. Layer with remaining omelet. Top omelet with remaining cottage cheese and tomato. Bake at 425°F for 5 to 7 minutes or until heated through. Garnish with parsley. Cut into wedges to serve.   *Makes 4 servings*

Nutrition information per serving:					
Calories	124	Total Fat	3 g	Sodium	363 mg
Cholesterol	3 mg	Saturated Fat	1 g	Dietary Fiber	2 g

Triple-Decker Vegetable Omelet

Morning Breads & Muffins

CRANBERRY POPPY SEED LOAF

Prep Time: 20 minutes	Cook Time: 70 minutes

2½ cups all-purpose flour
¾ cup granulated sugar
2 tablespoons poppy seed
1 tablespoon baking powder
1 cup skim milk
⅓ cup Fleischmann's Margarine, melted

¼ cup EGG BEATERS
1 teaspoon vanilla extract
2 teaspoons grated lemon peel
1 cup fresh or frozen cranberries, chopped
Powdered Sugar Glaze, optional (recipe follows)

In large bowl, combine flour, granulated sugar, poppy seed and baking powder; set aside.

In small bowl, combine milk, margarine, Egg Beaters, vanilla and lemon peel. Stir milk mixture into flour mixture just until moistened. Stir in cranberries. Spread batter into greased 8½×4½×2¼-inch loaf pan. Bake at 350°F for 60 to 70 minutes or until toothpick inserted in center comes out clean. Cool in pan on wire rack. Drizzle with Powdered Sugar Glaze if desired.   *Makes 12 servings*

POWDERED SUGAR GLAZE: In small bowl, combine 1 cup powdered sugar and 5 to 6 teaspoons water until smooth.

Nutrition information per serving:

(without glaze)

Calories	216	Total Fat	6 g	Sodium	172 mg
Cholesterol	0 mg	Saturated Fat	1 g	Dietary Fiber	1 g

Cranberry Poppy Seed Loaf

CARROT PECAN MUFFINS

Prep Time: 25 minutes   Cook Time: 25 minutes

1¾ cups all-purpose flour
 1 teaspoon baking soda
 1 teaspoon ground cinnamon
 ¼ teaspoon ground nutmeg
 1 cup sweetened applesauce
 ½ cup firmly packed light brown
    sugar
 ⅓ cup Fleischmann's Margarine,
    melted

¼ cup EGG BEATERS
 1 cup shredded carrots
 ½ cup pecan halves, chopped,
    divided
    Powdered Sugar Glaze (recipe
    follows)

In small bowl, combine flour, baking soda, cinnamon and nutmeg; set aside.

In large bowl, combine applesauce, brown sugar, margarine and Egg Beaters. Stir in flour mixture, carrots and ⅓ cup pecans just until moistened. Spoon batter into 12 lightly greased 2½-inch muffin-pan cups. Bake at 350°F for 20 to 25 minutes or until lightly browned. Cool on wire rack. Drizzle tops of muffins with Powdered Sugar Glaze; sprinkle with remaining pecans.   *Makes 1 dozen muffins*

POWDERED SUGAR GLAZE: In small bowl, combine 1 cup powdered sugar and 5 to 6 teaspoons water until smooth.

Nutrition information per serving:

(1 muffin)

Calories	236	Total Fat	8 g	Sodium	124 mg
Cholesterol	0 mg	Saturated Fat	1 g	Dietary Fiber	0 g

SPICY GINGERBREAD

Prep Time: 20 minutes   Cook Time: 1 hour

2 cups all-purpose flour
 1 cup light molasses
 ¾ cup buttermilk
 ½ cup granulated sugar
 ½ cup Fleischmann's Margarine,
    softened

¼ cup EGG BEATERS
 2 teaspoons baking soda
 1 teaspoon ground cinnamon
 ½ teaspoon ground ginger
 ¼ teaspoon ground cloves
    Powdered sugar, optional

In large bowl, with electric mixer at low speed, beat flour, molasses, buttermilk, granulated sugar, margarine, Egg Beaters, baking soda, cinnamon, ginger and cloves until moistened; scrape down side and bottom of bowl. Beat at medium speed for 3 minutes. Spread batter into greased 9-inch square baking pan. Bake at 350°F for 1 hour or until toothpick inserted in center comes out clean. Cool in pan on wire rack. Dust with powdered sugar before serving if desired. Cut into 16 (2-inch) squares. *Makes 16 servings*

Nutrition information per serving:

(without powdered sugar)

Calories	194	Total Fat	6 g	Sodium	164 mg
Cholesterol	0 mg	Saturated Fat	1 g	Dietary Fiber	0 g

ORANGE CRUMB APPLE MUFFINS

Prep Time: 25 minutes   Cook Time: 25 minutes

1½ cups all-purpose flour
 1 tablespoon baking powder
½ teaspoon ground cinnamon
⅓ cup firmly packed light brown
    sugar
¼ cup Fleischmann's Margarine,
    melted

½ cup milk
¼ cup EGG BEATERS
¼ cup low fat vanilla yogurt
¾ cup peeled and chopped apple
    Orange Crumb Topping
    (recipe follows)

In small bowl, combine flour, baking powder and cinnamon; set aside.

In medium bowl, with electric mixer at medium speed, beat sugar and margarine until creamy. Blend in milk, Egg Beaters and yogurt until smooth. Stir in flour mixture and apple just until moistened. Spoon batter into 12 lightly greased 2½-inch muffin-pan cups; sprinkle with Orange Crumb Topping. Bake at 400°F for 25 minutes or until lightly browned. Serve warm. *Makes 1 dozen muffins*

ORANGE CRUMB TOPPING: In small bowl, combine 2 tablespoons all-purpose flour, 2 tablespoons firmly packed light brown sugar and ½ teaspoon grated orange peel. Cut in 1 tablespoon Fleischmann's Margarine until crumbly.

Nutrition information per serving:

(1 muffin)

Calories	153	Total Fat	5 g	Sodium	186 mg
Cholesterol	2 mg	Saturated Fat	1 g	Dietary Fiber	1 g

BLUEBERRY KUCHEN

Prep Time: 20 minutes   Cook Time: 35 minutes

1½ cups all-purpose flour
 2 teaspoons baking powder
 ½ cup EGG BEATERS
 ⅓ cup skim milk
 1 teaspoon vanilla extract
 ½ cup granulated sugar
 ¼ cup Fleischmann's Margarine,
    softened

1 (21-ounce) can blueberry pie
    filling and topping
 Streusel Topping (recipe
    follows)
 Powdered Sugar Glaze,
    optional (recipe follows)

In small bowl, combine flour and baking powder; set aside. In another small bowl, combine Egg Beaters, milk and vanilla; set aside.

In medium bowl, with electric mixer at medium speed, beat granulated sugar and margarine until creamy. Alternately add flour mixture and egg mixture, blending well after each addition. Spread batter into greased 9-inch square baking pan.

Bake at 350°F for 20 minutes. Spoon blueberry pie filling over batter; sprinkle Streusel Topping over filling. Bake for 10 to 15 minutes more or until toothpick inserted in center comes out clean. Cool in pan on wire rack. Drizzle with Powdered Sugar Glaze if desired. Cut into 12 (3×2-inch) pieces.   *Makes 12 servings*

STREUSEL TOPPING: In small bowl, combine 3 tablespoons all-purpose flour, 3 tablespoons powdered sugar and ¼ teaspoon ground cinnamon. Cut in 1 tablespoon Fleischmann's Margarine until crumbly.

POWDERED SUGAR GLAZE: In small bowl, combine 1 cup powdered sugar and 5 to 6 teaspoons water until smooth.

Nutrition information per serving:					
		(without glaze)			
Calories	227	Total Fat	5 g	Sodium	147 mg
Cholesterol	0 mg	Saturated Fat	1 g	Dietary Fiber	0 g

Blueberry Kuchen

CINNAMON–BLUEBERRY MUFFINS

| Prep Time: 25 minutes | Cook Time: 18 minutes |

2 cups all-purpose flour
1/3 cup sugar
1 tablespoon baking powder
1/2 teaspoon grated lemon peel
1 cup skim milk
1/4 cup EGG BEATERS
1/3 cup plus 1 tablespoon
    Fleischmann's Margarine,
    melted, divided

3/4 cup fresh or frozen blueberries
    or cranberries*
Cinnamon Topping (recipe
    follows)

In large bowl, combine flour, sugar, baking powder and lemon peel; set aside.

In medium bowl, combine milk, Egg Beaters and 1/3 cup melted margarine. Stir into flour mixture just until moistened; gently stir in blueberries or cranberries. Spoon batter into 12 lightly greased 2 1/2-inch muffin-pan cups. Bake at 400°F for 15 to 18 minutes or until lightly browned. Dip tops of warm muffins in remaining melted margarine, then in Cinnamon Topping. Serve warm.   *Makes 1 dozen muffins*

*If using cranberries, substitute grated orange peel for lemon peel.

CINNAMON TOPPING: In small bowl, combine 2 tablespoons sugar and 1/4 teaspoon ground cinnamon.

Nutrition information per serving:

(1 muffin)

| Calories | 197 | Total Fat | 7 g | Sodium | 186 mg |
| Cholesterol | 0 mg | Saturated Fat | 1 g | Dietary Fiber | 1 g |

APPLE STREUSEL COFFEECAKE

Prep Time: 20 minutes   Cook Time: 35 minutes

1½ cups all-purpose flour
2 teaspoons baking powder
½ cup EGG BEATERS
⅓ cup skim milk
1 teaspoon vanilla extract
½ cup granulated sugar
¼ cup Fleischmann's Margarine,
    softened

1½ cups chopped apples
    Streusel Topping (recipe
      follows)
    Powdered Sugar Glaze,
      optional (recipe follows)

In small bowl, combine flour and baking powder; set aside. In another small bowl, combine Egg Beaters, milk and vanilla; set aside.

In medium bowl, with electric mixer at medium speed, beat granulated sugar and margarine until creamy. Alternately add flour mixture and egg mixture, blending well after each addition. Spread batter into greased 9-inch round cake pan. Arrange apple pieces over top, gently pressing into batter.

Bake at 350°F for 20 minutes. Sprinkle top with Streusel Topping. Bake for 10 to 15 minutes more or until toothpick inserted in center comes out clean. Cool in pan on wire rack. Drizzle with Powdered Sugar Glaze if desired.

Makes 12 servings

STREUSEL TOPPING: In small bowl, combine 3 tablespoons all-purpose flour, 3 tablespoons powdered sugar and ¾ teaspoon ground cinnamon. Cut in 2 tablespoons Fleischmann's Margarine until crumbly.

POWDERED SUGAR GLAZE: In small bowl, combine 1 cup powdered sugar and 5 to 6 teaspoons water until smooth.

Nutrition information per serving:

(without glaze)

Calories	174	Total Fat	6 g	Sodium	122 mg
Cholesterol	0 mg	Saturated Fat	1 g	Dietary Fiber	1 g

LEMON POPPY SEED MUFFINS

Prep Time: 15 minutes   **Cook Time: 22 minutes**

2½ cups all-purpose flour
½ cup sugar
2 tablespoons poppy seed
1 tablespoon baking powder
1¼ cups skim milk

¼ cup Fleischmann's Margarine, melted
¼ cup EGG BEATERS
1 tablespoon grated lemon peel

In large bowl, combine flour, sugar, poppy seed and baking powder; set aside.

In small bowl, combine milk, margarine, Egg Beaters and lemon peel. Stir into flour mixture just until moistened. Spoon batter into 12 lightly greased 2½-inch muffin-pan cups.* Bake at 400°F for 20 to 22 minutes or until lightly browned. Serve warm.   *Makes 1 dozen muffins*

*For miniature muffins, use 36 (1½-inch) muffin-pan cups. Reduce baking time to 14 to 16 minutes.

Nutrition information per serving:

(1 [2½-inch] or 3 [1½-inch] muffins)

Calories	189	Total Fat	6 g	Sodium	189 mg
Cholesterol	1 mg	Saturated Fat	1 g	Dietary Fiber	1 g

APPLESAUCE MOLASSES SNACKING CAKE

Prep Time: 25 minutes   **Cook Time: 25 minutes**

1½ cups all-purpose flour
1 cup whole wheat flour
1 teaspoon baking soda
1 teaspoon ground cinnamon
¼ teaspoon ground allspice
1 cup firmly packed dark brown sugar

½ cup Fleischmann's Margarine, softened
1¼ cups sweetened applesauce
½ cup EGG BEATERS
⅓ cup light molasses
½ cup seedless raisins
Powdered sugar, optional

In medium bowl, combine all-purpose flour, whole wheat flour, baking soda, cinnamon and allspice; set aside.

In large bowl, with electric mixer at medium speed, beat brown sugar and margarine until creamy. Add applesauce, Egg Beaters and molasses; beat until smooth. Gradually add flour mixture, beating until well blended. Stir in raisins. Spread batter into ungreased 15×10×1-inch baking pan. Bake at 350°F for 20 to 25 minutes or until toothpick inserted in center comes out clean. Cool in pan on wire rack. Dust with powdered sugar before serving if desired. Cut into 48 (2×1-inch) bars.   *Makes 4 dozen bars*

Nutrition information per serving:

(1 bar without powdered sugar)

Calories	73	Total Fat	2 g	Sodium	39 mg
Cholesterol	0 mg	Saturated Fat	0 g	Dietary Fiber	0 mg

POCKET FULL OF JELLY MUFFINS

Prep Time: 25 minutes   Cook Time: 20 minutes

2 cups all-purpose flour
1 teaspoon baking powder
¼ teaspoon baking soda
⅓ cup honey
¼ cup Fleischmann's Margarine, melted
¾ cup orange juice
6 tablespoons EGG BEATERS, divided

2 teaspoons grated orange peel
¼ cup sliced almonds, finely chopped
1 tablespoon sugar
½ teaspoon ground cinnamon
⅓ cup jelly, any flavor

In small bowl, combine flour, baking powder and baking soda; set aside.

In large bowl, combine honey and margarine; blend in orange juice, 4 tablespoons Egg Beaters and orange peel. Stir in flour mixture just until moistened. Spoon batter into 12 lightly greased 2½-inch muffin-pan cups. Brush remaining Egg Beaters over tops of batter. In small bowl, combine almonds, sugar and cinnamon; sprinkle over batter. Bake at 375°F for 20 minutes or until lightly browned.

While muffins are still warm, poke hole in top center, halfway into each muffin; fill each with a teaspoonful of jelly. Serve warm.

Makes 1 dozen muffins

Nutrition Information per serving:

(1 muffin)

Calories	193	Total Fat	5 g	Sodium	88 mg
Cholesterol	0 mg	Saturated Fat	1 g	Dietary Fiber	1 g

Brunches & Lunches

HONEY–DIJON SALAD WITH SHRIMP

Prep Time: 25 minutes

8 cups torn romaine lettuce
    leaves
1 pound large shrimp, cleaned
    and cooked
3 cups sliced mushrooms
2 cups sliced carrots
½ cup EGG BEATERS

¼ cup corn oil
¼ cup white wine vinegar
¼ cup Dijon-style mustard
¼ cup honey
2 cups plain croutons, optional
    Carrot curls, for garnish

In large bowl, combine lettuce, shrimp, mushrooms and sliced carrots; set aside.

In small bowl, whisk together Egg Beaters, oil, vinegar, mustard and honey until well blended. To serve, pour dressing over salad, tossing until well coated. Top with croutons if desired. Garnish with carrot curls.

Makes 8 servings

Nutrition information per serving:

(with croutons)

Calories	252	Total Fat	9 g	Sodium	538 mg
Cholesterol	111 mg	Saturated Fat	1 g	Dietary Fiber	2 g

Honey-Dijon Salad with Shrimp

MINI VEGETABLE QUICHES

Prep Time: 25 minutes   Cook Time: 30 minutes

2 cups cut-up vegetables (bell
    peppers, broccoli, zucchini
    and/or carrots)
2 tablespoons chopped green
    onions
2 tablespoons Fleischmann's
    Margarine

4 (8-inch) flour tortillas, each
    cut into 8 triangles
1 cup EGG BEATERS
1 cup skim milk
½ teaspoon dried basil leaves

In medium nonstick skillet, over medium-high heat, sauté vegetables and
green onions in margarine until tender.

Arrange 4 tortilla pieces in each of 8 (6-ounce) greased custard cups or
ramekins, placing points of tortilla pieces at center of bottom of cup and
pressing lightly to form shape of cup. Divide vegetable mixture evenly
among cups. In small bowl, combine Egg Beaters, milk and basil. Pour
evenly over vegetable mixture. Place cups on baking sheet. Bake at 375°F
for 20 to 25 minutes or until puffed and knife inserted into centers comes
out clean. Let stand 5 minutes before serving.   *Makes 8 servings*

Nutrition information per serving:					
Calories	122	Total Fat	4 g	Sodium	198 mg
Cholesterol	1 mg	Saturated Fat	1 g	Dietary Fiber	1 g

Mini Vegetable Quiches

NOODLES THAI STYLE

Prep Time: 25 minutes   **Cook Time: 5 minutes**

¼ cup ketchup
2 tablespoons reduced-sodium
    soy sauce
1 tablespoon sugar
¼ to ½ teaspoon crushed red
    pepper
¼ teaspoon ground ginger
2 teaspoons Fleischmann's
    Margarine, divided
1 cup EGG BEATERS

8 green onions, cut in 1½-inch
    pieces
1 clove garlic, minced
¾ pound fresh bean sprouts,
    rinsed and well drained
8 ounces linguine, cooked and
    drained
¼ cup dry roasted unsalted
    peanuts, chopped

In small bowl, combine ketchup, soy sauce, sugar, pepper and ginger; set aside.

In large nonstick skillet, over medium heat, melt 1 teaspoon margarine. Pour Egg Beaters into skillet. Cook, stirring occasionally until set. Remove to another small bowl.

In same skillet, over medium heat, sauté green onions and garlic in remaining margarine for 2 minutes. Stir in bean sprouts; cook for 2 minutes. Stir in ketchup mixture. Cook until heated through. Transfer to large bowl; add eggs and linguine. Toss until combined. Top with peanuts.

Makes 6 (1-cup) servings

Nutrition information per serving:

Calories	250	Total Fat	5 g	Sodium	394 mg
Cholesterol	0 mg	Saturated Fat	1 g	Dietary Fiber	3 g

MEXICAN STRATA OLÉ

Prep Time: 25 minutes   **Cook Time: 50 minutes**

4 (6-inch) corn tortillas, halved,
    divided
1 cup chopped onion
½ cup chopped green bell
    pepper
1 clove garlic, crushed
1 teaspoon dried oregano leaves
½ teaspoon ground cumin
1 teaspoon Fleischmann's
    Margarine

1 cup dried kidney beans,
    cooked in unsalted water
    according to package
    directions
½ cup (2 ounces) shredded
    reduced-fat Cheddar cheese
1½ cups skim milk
1 cup EGG BEATERS
1 cup thick and chunky salsa

Arrange half the tortilla pieces in bottom of greased 12×8×2-inch baking dish; set aside.

In large nonstick skillet, over medium-high heat, sauté onion, bell pepper, garlic, oregano and cumin in margarine until tender; stir in beans. Spoon half the mixture over tortillas; repeat layers once. Sprinkle with cheese.

In medium bowl, combine milk and Egg Beaters; pour evenly over cheese. Bake at 350°F for 40 minutes or until puffed and golden brown. Let stand 10 minutes before serving. Serve topped with salsa.   *Makes 8 servings*

Nutrition information per serving:

Calories	142	Total Fat	3 g	Sodium	293 mg
Cholesterol	1 mg	Saturated Fat	0 g	Dietary Fiber	0 g

SPINACH–CHEDDAR SQUARES

Prep Time: 15 minutes   Cook Time: 40 minutes

1½ cups EGG BEATERS
¾ cup skim milk
1 tablespoon dried onion flakes
1 tablespoon grated Parmesan cheese
¼ teaspoon garlic powder
⅛ teaspoon ground black pepper

¼ cup plain dry bread crumbs
¾ cup shredded fat-free Cheddar cheese, divided
1 (10-ounce) package frozen chopped spinach, thawed and well drained
¼ cup diced pimientos

In medium bowl, combine Egg Beaters, milk, onion flakes, Parmesan cheese, garlic powder and pepper; set aside.

Sprinkle bread crumbs evenly into bottom of lightly greased 8×8×2-inch baking dish. Top with ½ cup Cheddar cheese and spinach. Pour egg mixture evenly over spinach; top with remaining Cheddar cheese and pimientos.

Bake at 350°F for 35 to 40 minutes or until knife inserted in center comes out clean. Let stand 10 minutes before serving.

Makes 16 appetizer servings

Nutrition information per serving:

Calories	39	Total Fat	0 g	Sodium	134 mg
Cholesterol	1 mg	Saturated Fat	0 g	Dietary Fiber	0 g

RATATOUILLE STUFFED ZUCCHINI

Prep Time: 25 minutes   **Cook Time: 35 minutes**

2 medium zucchini
½ cup chopped onion
1 clove garlic, minced
1 tablespoon Fleischmann's
    Margarine, divided
½ cup chopped green bell pepper
½ cup chopped peeled eggplant
½ cup chopped tomato

¼ cup EGG BEATERS
1 teaspoon dried basil leaves
19 low-salt round buttery
    crackers, divided
1 tablespoon grated Parmesan
    cheese

Halve each zucchini lengthwise; scoop out center portions, leaving ¼-inch shell. Chop 1 cup scooped out zucchini filling; reserve.

In large nonstick skillet, over medium heat, sauté onion and garlic in 2 teaspoons margarine until tender. Stir in bell pepper, eggplant, tomato and reserved chopped zucchini; cook until tender-crisp, about 5 minutes. Remove from heat; stir in Egg Beaters and basil.

Coarsely break 15 crackers; stir into vegetable mixture. Spoon vegetable mixture into zucchini shells. Place zucchini shells in 12×8×2-inch baking dish.

Melt remaining margarine. Crush remaining crackers; in small bowl, toss with melted margarine until well coated. Stir in cheese; sprinkle over vegetable mixture. Bake at 375°F for 20 to 25 minutes or until hot.

Makes 4 servings

Nutrition information per serving:

Calories	152	Total Fat	8 g	Sodium	144 mg
Cholesterol	1 mg	Saturated Fat	1 g	Dietary Fiber	1 g

Ratatouille Stuffed Zucchini

VEGETABLE STRATA

Prep Time: 15 minutes   **Cook Time: 55 minutes**

2 slices white bread, cubed
¼ cup shredded reduced-fat
    Swiss cheese
½ cup sliced carrots
½ cup sliced mushrooms
¼ cup chopped onion
1 clove garlic, crushed

1 teaspoon Fleischmann's
    Margarine
½ cup chopped tomato
½ cup snow peas
1 cup EGG BEATERS
¾ cup skim milk

Place bread cubes evenly into bottom of greased 1½-quart casserole dish. Sprinkle with cheese; set aside.

In medium nonstick skillet, over medium heat, sauté carrots, mushrooms, onion and garlic in margarine until tender. Stir in tomato and snow peas; cook 1 to 2 minutes more. Spoon over cheese. In small bowl, combine Egg Beaters and milk; pour over vegetable mixture. Bake at 375°F for 45 to 50 minutes or until knife inserted in center comes out clean. Let stand 10 minutes before serving.   *Makes 6 servings*

Nutritional information per serving:

Calories	94	Total Fat	2 g	Sodium	161 mg
Cholesterol	3 mg	Saturated Fat	1 g	Dietary Fiber	1 g

EGG SALAD SANDWICHES

Prep Time: 20 minutes

1 cup EGG BEATERS, hard-
    cooked and chopped
    (see page 7)
¼ cup chopped celery
¼ cup chopped onion
2 tablespoons fat-free
    mayonnaise

12 slices whole wheat bread,
    divided
6 lettuce leaves
1 large tomato, cut into 6 thin
    slices

In small bowl, combine hard-cooked Egg Beaters, celery, onion and mayonnaise. On each of 6 bread slices, place lettuce leaf and tomato slice; top each with about ¼ cup egg salad and remaining bread slice.
                    Makes 6 servings

Nutrition information per serving:

Calories	173	Total Fat	2 g	Sodium	408 mg
Cholesterol	0 mg	Saturated Fat	1 g	Dietary Fiber	4 g

Vegetable Strata

INTERNATIONAL TATER TOPPERS

Prep Time: 20 minutes   Cook Time: 20 minutes

2 teaspoons Fleischmann's
    Margarine
1 cup EGG BEATERS
4 medium baking potatoes
    (about 5½ ounces each),
    baked and split open

**International Toppings (recipes
follow)**

In 8-inch nonstick skillet, over medium heat, melt margarine. Pour Egg
Beaters into skillet. Cook, stirring occasionally until set. Spoon into
potatoes; top with desired International Topping. Serve immediately.

Makes 4 servings

ITALIAN TOPPING: In small skillet, over medium-high heat, sauté
1 large tomato, chopped (about 1½ cups), ⅓ cup chopped green bell
pepper, ⅓ cup chopped onion, 1 clove garlic, crushed, and 1 teaspoon
Italian seasoning in 1 tablespoon Fleischmann's Margarine for 2 to 3
minutes. Stir in ⅓ cup low-sodium chicken broth. Simmer, uncovered, for
3 to 4 minutes.

Nutrition information per serving:					
Calories	212	Total Fat	5 g	Sodium	173 mg
Cholesterol	0 mg	Saturated Fat	1 g	Dietary Fiber	3 g

MEXICAN TOPPING: In medium skillet, over medium-high heat,
sauté ½ cup chopped onion, ½ cup chopped zucchini, ½ teaspoon
ground cumin and ⅛ teaspoon crushed red pepper in 1 tablespoon
Fleischmann's Margarine until tender. Add 1 (10-ounce) can reduced-
sodium tomatoes, chopped. Cook, stirring occasionally for 3 to 4 minutes
or until slightly thickened.

Nutrition information per serving:					
Calories	211	Total Fat	5 g	Sodium	163 mg
Cholesterol	0 mg	Saturated Fat	1 g	Dietary Fiber	3 g

(continued on page 54)

*Top to bottom: International Tater Topper
with French Topping (page 54), International Tater
Topper with Mexican Topping*

International Tater Toppers, continued

INDIAN TOPPING: In small bowl, combine 1 cup low fat plain yogurt, 2 tablespoons sliced green onions, 1 tablespoon chutney and ½ teaspoon curry powder.

Nutrition information per serving:					
Calories	208	Total Fat	2 g	Sodium	175 mg
Cholesterol	3 mg	Saturated Fat	1 g	Dietary Fiber	2 g

FRENCH TOPPING: In medium skillet, over medium-high heat, sauté 1 cup sliced mushrooms, 1 small red onion, sliced, 1 small carrot, julienned, and 1 clove garlic, crushed, in 1 tablespoon Fleischmann's Margarine until tender. Stir in 1 tablespoon all-purpose flour; cook 1 minute. Add 1 cup dry red wine. Cook, stirring occasionally for 4 to 5 minutes or until thickened.

Nutrition information per serving:					
Calories	258	Total Fat	5 g	Sodium	162 mg
Cholesterol	0 mg	Saturated Fat	1 g	Dietary Fiber	3 g

CAESAR SALAD

Prep Time: 15 minutes

12 cups torn romaine lettuce
  leaves
½ cup EGG BEATERS
¼ cup olive oil*
¼ cup lemon juice

1 teaspoon Dijon-style mustard
2 cloves garlic, minced
¼ teaspoon ground black pepper
  Grated Parmesan cheese,
  optional

Place lettuce in large bowl; set aside.

In small bowl, whisk together Egg Beaters, oil, lemon juice, mustard, garlic and pepper until well blended. To serve, pour dressing over lettuce, tossing until well coated. Serve with Parmesan cheese if desired.

Makes 8 servings

*Vegetable oil can be substituted.

Nutrition information per serving:					
		(without cheese)			
Calories	84	Total Fat	7 g	Sodium	48 mg
Cholesterol	0 mg	Saturated Fat	1 g	Dietary Fiber	1 g

SPINACH QUICHE

Prep Time: 30 minutes   Cook Time: 50 minutes

½ cup chopped onion
1 clove garlic, crushed
1 teaspoon Fleischmann's
  Margarine
1 (10-ounce) package frozen
  chopped spinach, thawed
  and well drained

1 (9-inch) pastry crust, unbaked
1 cup EGG BEATERS
1 cup skim milk
1 tablespoon all-purpose flour
1 teaspoon dried basil leaves
¾ teaspoon liquid hot pepper
  seasoning

In medium nonstick skillet, over medium-high heat, sauté onion and garlic in margarine until tender; add spinach. Spoon into bottom of pie crust; set aside.

In small bowl, combine Egg Beaters, milk, flour, basil and liquid hot pepper seasoning; pour evenly over spinach mixture. Bake at 350°F for 45 to 50 minutes or until knife inserted in center comes out clean. Let stand 10 minutes before serving.   *Makes 8 servings*

Nutrition information per serving:

Calories	156	Total Fat	8 g	Sodium	234 mg
Cholesterol	1 mg	Saturated Fat	2 g	Dietary Fiber	0 g

SALMON QUICHE: Prepare as above substituting 1 (7¾-ounce) can low-sodium salmon, drained and flaked, for spinach and 1 teaspoon dried dill weed for basil. Omit liquid hot pepper seasoning.

Nutrition information per serving:

Calories	181	Total Fat	10 g	Sodium	212 mg
Cholesterol	10 mg	Saturated Fat	2 g	Dietary Fiber	0 g

ORANGE AND RED ONION SALAD

Prep Time: 25 minutes

¼ cup EGG BEATERS
2 tablespoons white wine
   vinegar
¼ teaspoon paprika
⅓ cup vegetable oil
2 tablespoons honey

2 tablespoons orange juice
6 cups torn romaine lettuce and
   fresh spinach leaves
1 cup orange segments
⅓ cup thinly sliced red onion

In electric blender container, blend Egg Beaters, vinegar and paprika just until mixed. Without turning off blender, pour in oil in a slow steady stream. Continue blending until oil is completely incorporated and mixture is smooth and thick. Pour into medium bowl; stir in honey and orange juice. Cover; chill until ready to use.

In large bowl, combine lettuce and spinach leaves, orange segments and onion. To serve, pour dressing over salad, tossing until well coated.

Makes 6 servings

Nutrition information per serving:

Calories	164	Total Fat	12 g	Sodium	42 mg
Cholesterol	0 mg	Saturated Fat	2 g	Dietary Fiber	2 g

HUEVOS RANCHWICH

Prep Time: 10 minutes   **Cook Time: 5 minutes**

¼ cup EGG BEATERS
1 teaspoon diced green chiles
1 whole wheat hamburger roll,
   split and toasted

1 tablespoon thick and chunky
   salsa, heated
1 tablespoon shredded reduced-
   fat Cheddar and Monterey
   Jack cheese blend

On lightly greased griddle or skillet, pour Egg Beaters into lightly greased 4-inch egg ring or biscuit cutter. Sprinkle with chiles. Cook 2 to 3 minutes or until bottom of egg patty is set. Remove egg ring and turn egg patty over. Cook 1 to 2 minutes longer or until done.

To serve, place egg patty on bottom of roll. Top with salsa, cheese and roll top.

Makes 1 sandwich

Nutrition information per serving:

Calories	143	Total Fat	2 g	Sodium	411 mg
Cholesterol	6 mg	Saturated Fat	1 g	Dietary Fiber	0 g

Orange and Red Onion Salad

Dinnertime Delights

STUFFED SHELLS FLORENTINE

Prep Time: 30 minutes   Cook Time: 40 minutes

1 cup (about 4 ounces) coarsely
  chopped mushrooms
½ cup chopped onion
1 clove garlic, minced
1 teaspoon Italian seasoning
¼ teaspoon ground black pepper
1 tablespoon Fleischmann's
  Margarine
1 (16-ounce) container fat-free
  cottage cheese

1 (10-ounce) package frozen
  chopped spinach, thawed
  and well drained
½ cup EGG BEATERS
24 jumbo pasta shells, cooked in
  unsalted water and drained
1 (15¼-ounce) jar reduced-
  sodium spaghetti sauce,
  divided

In large skillet, over medium-high heat, sauté mushrooms, onion, garlic,
Italian seasoning and pepper in margarine until tender. Remove from heat;
stir in cottage cheese, spinach and Egg Beaters. Spoon mixture into shells.

Spread ½ cup spaghetti sauce in bottom of 13×9×2-inch baking dish;
arrange shells over sauce. Top with remaining sauce; cover. Bake at 350°F
for 35 minutes or until hot.   *Makes 8 servings*

Nutrition information per serving:					
Calories	229	Total Fat	5 g	Sodium	549 mg
Cholesterol	3 mg	Saturated Fat	1 g	Dietary Fiber	3 g

Stuffed Shells Florentine

CHICKEN FLORENTINE WITH LEMON MUSTARD SAUCE

Prep Time: 25 minutes   Cook Time: 15 minutes

2 whole boneless skinless
　 chicken breasts, halved
　 (1 pound)
¼ cup EGG BEATERS
½ cup plain dry bread crumbs
1 teaspoon dried basil leaves
1 teaspoon garlic powder
2 tablespoons Fleischmann's
　 Sweet Unsalted Margarine,
　 divided

⅓ cup water
2 tablespoons Dijon-style
　 mustard
2 tablespoons lemon juice
1 tablespoon sugar
1 (10-ounce) package frozen
　 chopped spinach, cooked,
　 well drained and kept warm

Pound chicken breasts to ¼-inch thickness. Pour Egg Beaters into shallow bowl. Combine bread crumbs, basil and garlic. Dip chicken breasts into Egg Beaters, then coat with bread crumb mixture.

In large nonstick skillet, over medium-high heat, melt 1 tablespoon margarine. Add chicken; cook for 5 to 7 minutes on each side or until browned and no longer pink in center. Remove chicken from skillet; keep warm. In same skillet, melt remaining margarine; stir in water, mustard, lemon juice and sugar. Simmer 1 minute or until thickened. To serve, arrange chicken on serving platter. Top with spinach; drizzle with lemon-mustard sauce. Garnish as desired.   *Makes 4 servings*

Nutrition information per serving:

Calories	278	Total Fat	8 g	Sodium	468 mg
Cholesterol	69 mg	Saturated Fat	2 g	Dietary Fiber	0 g

Chicken Florentine with Lemon Mustard Sauce

PENNE PRIMAVERA

Prep Time: 25 minutes   Cook Time: 10 minutes

2 cups red, green or yellow bell
   pepper strips
1 cup sliced zucchini or yellow
   squash
1 cup julienne carrot strips
½ cup sliced onion
2 teaspoons Italian seasoning
2 cloves garlic, crushed

¼ teaspoon ground black pepper
2 tablespoons Fleischmann's
   Margarine
1 cup coarsely chopped tomato
1 pound penne pasta, cooked in
   unsalted water and drained
1 cup EGG BEATERS
¼ cup grated Parmesan cheese

In large skillet, over medium heat, sauté bell peppers, zucchini, carrots, onion, Italian seasoning, garlic and black pepper in margarine for 3 minutes. Add tomato; sauté for 1 minute more or until vegetables are tender-crisp. Toss with hot pasta, Egg Beaters and cheese.

Makes 8 servings

Nutrition information per serving:

Calories	288	Total Fat	5 g	Sodium	140 mg
Cholesterol	2 mg	Saturated Fat	1 g	Dietary Fiber	3 g

SPINACH CHEESE ROULADE

Prep Time: 30 minutes   Cook Time: 25 minutes

4 teaspoons Fleischmann's
   Margarine, divided
2 tablespoons all-purpose flour
1 cup skim milk
2 cups EGG BEATERS
1 medium onion, chopped
1 (10-ounce) package fresh
   spinach, coarsely chopped

½ cup low fat cottage cheese
   (1% milkfat)
1 (8-ounce) can no-salt-added
   tomato sauce
½ teaspoon dried basil leaves
½ teaspoon garlic powder

In small saucepan, over medium heat, melt 3 teaspoons margarine; blend in flour. Cook, stirring until smooth and bubbly; remove from heat. Gradually blend in milk; return to heat. Heat to a boil, stirring constantly until thickened; cool slightly. Stir in Egg Beaters. Spread mixture in bottom of 15½×10½×1-inch baking pan that has been greased, lined with foil and greased again. Bake at 350°F for 20 minutes or until set.

In medium skillet, sauté onion in remaining margarine until tender. Add spinach and cook until wilted, about 3 minutes; stir in cottage cheese. Keep warm.

Invert egg mixture onto large piece of foil. Spread with spinach mixture; roll up from short end. In small saucepan, combine tomato sauce, basil and garlic; heat until warm. To serve, slice roll into 8 pieces; top with warm sauce.   *Makes 8 servings*

Nutrition information per serving:

Calories	95	Total Fat	3 g	Sodium	202 mg
Cholesterol	1 mg	Saturated Fat	1 g	Dietary Fiber	1 g

SPICY CHICKEN BURRITOS

Prep Time: 20 minutes   Cook Time: 20 minutes

1 medium onion, halved and sliced
1 small green bell pepper, diced
1 tablespoon Fleischmann's Margarine
½ pound shredded cooked chicken (1¼ cups)
1 medium tomato, diced
1½ cups EGG BEATERS

½ teaspoon seasoned pepper
¼ teaspoon garlic powder
½ cup (2 ounces) shredded reduced-fat Cheddar cheese
6 (10-inch) flour tortillas, warmed
½ cup thick and chunky salsa
Additional thick and chunky salsa, optional

In large nonstick skillet, over medium heat, sauté onion and bell pepper in margarine until tender. Add chicken and tomato; stir until heated through. Remove from skillet; keep warm.

In same skillet, over medium heat, cook Egg Beaters, seasoned pepper and garlic powder, stirring occasionally until mixture is set. Stir in chicken mixture; sprinkle with cheese. Evenly divide and spoon mixture onto warm tortillas; top each with salsa. Fold two opposite ends of each tortilla over filling, then fold in sides like an envelope. Serve with additional salsa if desired.   *Makes 6 servings*

Nutrition information per serving:

(without additional salsa)

Calories	349	Total Fat	10 g	Sodium	706 mg
Cholesterol	40 mg	Saturated Fat	3 g	Dietary Fiber	3 g

BROCCOLI LASAGNA BIANCA

Prep Time: 20 minutes   Cook Time: 90 minutes

1 (15- to 16-ounce) container
    fat-free ricotta cheese
1 cup EGG BEATERS
1 tablespoon minced basil
    (*or* 1 teaspoon dried basil
    leaves)
½ cup chopped onion
1 clove garlic, minced
2 tablespoons Fleischmann's
    Margarine
¼ cup all-purpose flour
2 cups skim milk

2 (10-ounce) packages frozen
    chopped broccoli, thawed
    and well drained
1 cup (4 ounces) shredded part-
    skim mozzarella cheese
9 lasagna noodles, cooked and
    drained
1 small tomato, chopped
2 tablespoons grated Parmesan
    cheese
Fresh basil leaves, for garnish

In medium bowl, combine ricotta cheese, Egg Beaters and minced basil; set aside.

In large saucepan, over medium heat, sauté onion and garlic in margarine until tender-crisp. Stir in flour; cook for 1 minute. Gradually stir in milk; cook, stirring until mixture thickens and begins to boil. Remove from heat; stir in broccoli and mozzarella cheese.

In lightly greased 13×9×2-inch baking dish, place 3 lasagna noodles; top with ⅓ each ricotta and broccoli mixtures. Repeat layers 2 more times. Top with tomato; sprinkle with Parmesan cheese. Bake at 350°F for 1 hour or until set. Let stand 10 minutes before serving. Garnish with basil leaves.

Makes 8 servings

Nutrition information per serving:

Calories	302	Total Fat	7 g	Sodium	291 mg
Cholesterol	10 mg	Saturated Fat	2 g	Dietary Fiber	2 g

Broccoli Lasagna Bianca

VEGETABLE LASAGNA

| Prep Time: 20 minutes | Cook Time: 45 minutes |

2 cups low fat cottage cheese
   (1% milkfat)
1 (10-ounce) package frozen
   chopped spinach, thawed
   and well drained
1 cup shredded carrots
½ cup EGG BEATERS
2 tablespoons minced onion
1 teaspoon Italian seasoning

2 cups no-salt-added spaghetti
   sauce, divided
9 lasagna noodles, cooked in
   unsalted water and drained
1 cup (4 ounces) shredded part-
   skim mozzarella cheese
2 tablespoons grated Parmesan
   cheese

In medium bowl, combine cottage cheese, spinach, carrots, Egg Beaters, onion and Italian seasoning; set aside.

Spread ½ cup spaghetti sauce in bottom of greased 13×9×2-inch baking dish. Top with 3 noodles and ⅓ each spinach mixture and remaining sauce. Repeat layers 2 more times. Sprinkle with mozzarella and Parmesan cheese; cover. Bake at 375°F for 20 minutes. Uncover; bake for 25 minutes more or until set. Let stand 10 minutes before serving.

Makes 8 servings

Nutrition information per serving:

Calories	271	Total Fat	8 g	Sodium	392 mg
Cholesterol	11 mg	Saturated Fat	2 g	Dietary Fiber	2 g

PARMESAN CHICKEN

| Prep Time: 15 minutes | Cook Time: 15 minutes |

2 whole boneless skinless
   chicken breasts, halved
   (1 pound)
¼ cup EGG BEATERS
½ cup plain dry bread crumbs
3 tablespoons grated Parmesan
   cheese

1 teaspoon dried oregano leaves
2 tablespoons all-purpose flour
1 clove garlic, crushed
3 tablespoons Fleischmann's
   Margarine
1 cup no-salt-added spaghetti
   sauce, heated

Pound chicken breasts to ¼-inch thickness. Pour Egg Beaters into shallow bowl. Combine bread crumbs, cheese and oregano. Coat chicken breasts with flour, dip into Egg Beaters, then coat with bread crumb mixture.

In large nonstick skillet, over medium-high heat, sauté garlic in margarine for 1 minute. Add chicken; cook for 5 to 7 minutes on each side or until browned and no longer pink in center. Serve warm with spaghetti sauce.

Makes 4 servings

Nutrition information per serving:					
Calories	344	Total Fat	15 g	Sodium	341 mg
Cholesterol	69 mg	Saturated Fat	3 g	Dietary Fiber	1 g

VEGETABLE–STUFFED TURKEY BREAST

Prep Time: 30 minutes   Cook Time: 2 hours

¾ **cup chopped onion**
2 **tablespoons Fleischmann's Margarine, divided**
1 **cup cooked regular long-grain rice**
1 **cup shredded carrots**

1 **cup sliced mushrooms**
½ **cup chopped fresh parsley**
¼ **cup EGG BEATERS**
½ **teaspoon poultry seasoning**
1 **whole turkey breast (about 5 pounds)**

In small skillet, over medium heat, sauté onion in 1 tablespoon margarine until tender; set aside.

In large bowl, combine rice, carrots, mushrooms, parsley, Egg Beaters and poultry seasoning; stir in onion. Remove skin from turkey breast. Place rice mixture into cavity of turkey breast; cover cavity with foil.

Place turkey, breast-side up, on rack in roasting pan. Melt remaining margarine; brush over turkey. Roast at 350°F according to package directions or until meat thermometer registers 170°F. If necessary, tent breast with foil after 30 minutes to prevent overbrowning. Let turkey stand 15 minutes before carving. Portion 3 ounces sliced turkey and ½ cup stuffing per serving. (Freeze remaining turkey for another use.)

Makes 8 servings

Nutrition information per serving:					
Calories	207	Total Fat	5 g	Sodium	99 mg
Cholesterol	59 mg	Saturated Fat	1 g	Dietary Fiber	1 g

SALMON STEAKS WITH LEMON DILL SAUCE

Prep Time: 15 minutes   **Cook Time: 15 minutes**

½ cup finely chopped red onion
2 teaspoons Fleischmann's
    Margarine
2 tablespoons all-purpose flour
1⅓ cups skim milk
½ cup EGG BEATERS

2 teaspoons grated lemon peel
¼ cup lemon juice
2 teaspoons dried dill weed
8 (½-inch-thick) salmon steaks
    (2 pounds)
Fresh dill sprigs, for garnish

In small saucepan, over low heat, sauté onion in margarine until tender-crisp. Stir in flour; cook for 1 minute. Over medium heat, gradually stir in milk; cook, stirring until mixture thickens and boils. Boil, stirring constantly, for 1 minute; remove from heat. Whisk in Egg Beaters, lemon peel, lemon juice and dried dill; return to heat. Cook, stirring constantly until thickened. *Do not boil.*

Meanwhile, grill or broil salmon steaks for 3 to 5 minutes on each side or until fish flakes easily when tested with fork. Top with sauce. Garnish with dill sprigs.   *Makes 8 servings*

Nutrition information per serving:

Calories	255	Total Fat	11 g	Sodium	118 mg
Cholesterol	83 mg	Saturated Fat	2 g	Dietary Fiber	0 g

LINGUINE WITH SPINACH PESTO

Prep Time: 15 minutes   **Cook Time: 10 minutes**

1 (10-ounce) package frozen
    chopped spinach, thawed
    and well drained
1 cup EGG BEATERS
⅓ cup walnut pieces
¼ cup grated Parmesan cheese

2 cloves garlic, crushed
1 pound thin linguine, cooked in
    unsalted water and drained
½ cup diced red bell pepper
Additional grated Parmesan
    cheese, optional

In electric blender container or food processor, blend spinach, Egg Beaters, walnuts, ¼ cup cheese and garlic until smooth. Toss with hot linguine and bell pepper. Top with additional cheese if desired.   *Makes 8 servings*

Nutrition information per serving:

(without additional cheese)

Calories	278	Total Fat	5 g	Sodium	119 mg
Cholesterol	2 mg	Saturated Fat	1 g	Dietary Fiber	2 g

Salmon Steak with Lemon Dill Sauce

CHICKEN FRIED RICE

Prep Time: 20 minutes   Cook Time: 30 minutes

½ cup sliced green onions
¼ cup sliced celery
¼ cup chopped red bell pepper
1 clove garlic, crushed
½ teaspoon grated gingerroot
¼ teaspoon crushed red pepper
   flakes
2 teaspoons peanut oil

6 tablespoons EGG BEATERS
3 cups cooked regular long-grain
   rice, prepared in unsalted
   water
2 cups cooked diced chicken
2 tablespoons reduced-sodium
   soy sauce
1 teaspoon sugar

In large nonstick skillet, over high heat, sauté green onions, celery, bell pepper, garlic, ginger and crushed red pepper in oil until tender-crisp. Pour Egg Beaters into skillet; cook, stirring occasionally until mixture is set. Stir in rice, chicken, soy sauce and sugar; cook until heated through.

Makes 6 servings

Nutrition information per serving:

Calories	253	Total Fat	5 g	Sodium	273 mg
Cholesterol	42 mg	Saturated Fat	1 g	Dietary Fiber	1 g

LEMON BASIL SAUCE

Prep Time: 5 minutes   Cook Time: 15 minutes

1 teaspoon Fleischmann's
   Margarine
2 teaspoons all-purpose flour
¼ cup skim milk

6 tablespoons EGG BEATERS
1 teaspoon grated lemon peel
1 teaspoon dried basil leaves

In small saucepan, over medium heat, melt margarine; blend in flour. Gradually add milk, stirring constantly with wire whisk until mixture thickens and begins to boil; remove from heat. Whisk in Egg Beaters, lemon peel and basil; return to heat. Cook, stirring constantly until thickened. *Do not boil.* Serve with fish, chicken or vegetables.

Makes ½ cup

Nutrition information per serving:

(2 tablespoons)

Calories	32	Total Fat	1 g	Sodium	56 mg
Cholesterol	0 mg	Saturated Fat	0 g	Dietary Fiber	0 g

Chicken Fried Rice

VARIATIONS OF HOLLANDAISE SAUCE

Prep Time: 10-20 minutes

6 tablespoons EGG BEATERS
2 tablespoons lemon juice
Dash ground red pepper

½ cup Fleischmann's Margarine,
melted and hot

ORIGINAL HOLLANDAISE SAUCE: In electric blender container, blend Egg Beaters, lemon juice and red pepper at medium speed just until mixed. Without turning off blender, pour in hot margarine in a slow steady stream. Continue blending until margarine is completely incorporated and mixture is smooth and thick. Mixture may be held in top of double boiler over hot (not boiling) water for up to 10 minutes before serving. Serve with vegetables, chicken or seafood.

Makes 1 cup

Nutrition information per serving:

(1 tablespoon)

Calories	54	Total Fat	5 g	Sodium	58 mg
Cholesterol	0 mg	Saturated Fat	1 g	Dietary Fiber	0 g

DIJON HOLLANDAISE SAUCE: Prepare as above, using ⅓ cup Egg Beaters and adding 1 tablespoon Dijon-style mustard to Egg Beaters mixture before blending. Serve with vegetables, chicken or seafood. Makes 1 cup.

Nutrition information per serving:

(1 tablespoon)

Calories	53	Total Fat	5 g	Sodium	82 mg
Cholesterol	0 mg	Saturated Fat	1 g	Dietary Fiber	0 g

BÉARNAISE SAUCE: Prepare as above, substituting ⅛ teaspoon white pepper for red pepper and adding 2 tablespoons chopped shallots, 2 sprigs fresh parsley and ¼ teaspoon dried tarragon leaves to Egg Beaters mixture before blending. Serve with beef or fish. Makes 1 cup.

Nutrition information per serving:

(1 tablespoon)

Calories	55	Total Fat	5 g	Sodium	59 mg
Cholesterol	0 mg	Saturated Fat	1 g	Dietary Fiber	0 g

PESTO SAUCE: Prepare as above, substituting ¼ teaspoon garlic powder for red pepper and adding 2 sprigs fresh parsley and 2 teaspoons dried basil leaves to Egg Beaters mixture before blending. Serve with vegetables or pasta. Makes 1 cup.

Nutrition information per serving:					
(1 tablespoon)					
Calories	55	Total Fat	5 g	Sodium	60 mg
Cholesterol	0 mg	Saturated Fat	1 g	Dietary Fiber	0 g

CHICKEN DIVAN

Prep Time: 20 minutes   Cook Time: 20 minutes

¾ **pound fresh or frozen asparagus spears, cooked**
1 **pound sliced cooked boneless skinless chicken breast**
2 **tablespoons Fleischmann's Margarine**
2 **tablespoons all-purpose flour**

1¾ **cups skim milk**
½ **cup EGG BEATERS**
2 **tablespoons sherry cooking wine**
¼ **teaspoon ground black pepper Paprika**

Arrange asparagus in bottom of greased 2-quart shallow baking dish. Place chicken slices over asparagus; cover with foil. Bake at 325°F for 20 minutes or until heated through.

In medium saucepan, over low heat, melt margarine; blend in flour. Cook, stirring until smooth and bubbly; remove from heat. Gradually blend in milk; return to heat. Heat to a boil, stirring constantly until thickened. Gradually blend half the hot milk mixture into Egg Beaters. Return mixture to saucepan; blend well. Stir in sherry and pepper. Spoon sauce over chicken and asparagus; sprinkle lightly with paprika.

Makes 4 servings

Nutrition information per serving:					
Calories	327	Total Fat	10 g	Sodium	277 mg
Cholesterol	99 mg	Saturated Fat	2 g	Dietary Fiber	3 g

Delicious Desserts

FRUIT TART

Prep Time: 30 minutes   Cook Time: 45 minutes

⅓ cup Fleischmann's Margarine
1¼ cups all-purpose flour
4 to 5 tablespoons ice water
1 cup EGG BEATERS

⅓ cup sugar
1 teaspoon vanilla extract
1¼ cups skim milk, scalded
1 cup sliced fresh fruit

In medium bowl, cut margarine into flour until mixture resembles coarse crumbs. Add water, 1 tablespoon at a time, tossing until moistened. Shape into a ball. On floured surface, roll dough into 11-inch circle, about ⅛ inch thick. Place in 9-inch pie plate, making a ½-inch-high fluted edge; set aside.

In medium bowl, combine Egg Beaters, sugar and vanilla; gradually stir in milk. Pour into prepared crust. Bake at 350°F for 45 to 50 minutes or until set. Cool completely on wire rack. Cover; chill until firm, about 2 hours. To serve, top with fruit.

Makes 10 servings

Nutrition information per serving:					
Calories	164	Total Fat	6 g	Sodium	47 mg
Cholesterol	1 mg	Saturated Fat	1 g	Dietary Fiber	1 g

Fruit Tart

CHOCOLATE CHEESECAKE

Prep Time: 30 minutes **Cook Time: 65 minutes**

24 chocolate wafers, finely
    crushed
2 to 3 tablespoons water
1 cup nonfat cottage cheese
½ cup EGG BEATERS
12 ounces light cream cheese
    (Neufchâtel), softened

1 cup granulated sugar
½ cup unsweetened cocoa
¼ cup all-purpose flour
1 teaspoon vanilla extract
¾ cup powdered sugar
¾ cup nonfat sour cream
Lavender flowers, for garnish

In small bowl, toss chocolate wafer crumbs with water, 1 tablespoon at a time, until crumbs are moistened. Press onto bottom of 8-inch springform pan; set aside.

In electric blender container or food processor, blend cottage cheese and Egg Beaters until smooth, scraping down sides of container as necessary. In large bowl, with electric mixer at medium speed, beat cream cheese and granulated sugar until smooth. Add cottage cheese mixture, cocoa, flour and vanilla; beat until well blended and smooth. Pour batter into prepared crust.

Bake at 300°F for 60 to 65 minutes or until puffed and set. Cool in pan on wire rack 15 minutes. Carefully run metal spatula around edge of cheesecake to loosen. Cover; chill at least 4 hours. In small bowl, combine powdered sugar and sour cream. Serve with cheesecake. Garnish with lavender.

Makes 12 servings

Nutrition information per serving:					
Calories	263	Total Fat	9 g	Sodium	308 mg
Cholesterol	23 mg	Saturated Fat	5 g	Dietary Fiber	1 g

Chocolate Cheesecake

SOFT APPLE CIDER COOKIES

Prep Time: 30 minutes   Cook Time: 12 minutes

1 cup firmly packed light brown sugar
½ cup Fleischmann's Margarine, softened
½ cup apple cider
½ cup EGG BEATERS
2¼ cups all-purpose flour

1½ teaspoons ground cinnamon
1 teaspoon baking soda
¼ teaspoon salt
2 medium apples, peeled and diced (about 1½ cups)
¾ cup almonds, chopped
Cider Glaze (recipe follows)

In large bowl, with electric mixer at medium speed, beat sugar and margarine until creamy. Add cider and Egg Beaters; beat until smooth. With electric mixer at low speed, gradually blend in flour, cinnamon, baking soda and salt. Stir in apples and almonds.

Drop dough by tablespoonfuls, 2 inches apart, onto greased baking sheets. Bake at 375°F for 10 to 12 minutes or until golden brown. Remove from sheets; cool on wire racks. Drizzle with Cider Glaze.

Makes 4 dozen cookies

CIDER GLAZE: In small bowl, combine 1 cup powdered sugar and 2 tablespoons apple cider until smooth.

Nutrition information per serving:

(1 cookie)

Calories	80	Total Fat	3 g	Sodium	50 mg
Cholesterol	0 mg	Saturated Fat	0 g	Dietary Fiber	0 g

ORANGE–BANANA NOG

Prep Time: 5 minutes

3 cups skim milk
1 cup EGG BEATERS
1 banana, cut up

⅓ cup frozen orange juice concentrate
¼ cup honey
1 tablespoon wheat germ

In electric blender container, blend milk, Egg Beaters, banana, orange juice concentrate, honey and wheat germ until smooth. Serve immediately.

Makes 6 (8-ounce) servings

Nutrition information per serving:

Calories	148	Total Fat	0 g	Sodium	115 mg
Cholesterol	2 mg	Saturated Fat	0 g	Dietary Fiber	1 g

FAT–FREE CHEESECAKE

Prep Time: 20 minutes   Cook Time: 50 minutes

1 tablespoon graham cracker
    crumbs
1½ cups nonfat cottage cheese
1 cup EGG BEATERS, divided

½ cup sugar
½ cup nonfat cream cheese
¼ teaspoon grated lemon peel
1 tablespoon lemon juice

Sprinkle graham cracker crumbs on bottom and up sides of lightly greased 9-inch square baking pan; set aside.

In electric blender container or food processor, blend cottage cheese and ½ cup Egg Beaters until smooth, scraping down sides of container as necessary.

In large bowl, with electric mixer at low speed, beat cottage cheese mixture, remaining Egg Beaters, sugar, cream cheese, lemon peel and lemon juice for 2 minutes. Pour into prepared pan. Bake at 325°F for 50 minutes or until set and lightly browned. Cool in pan on wire rack. Cover; chill at least 2 hours. To serve, cut into 9 (3-inch) squares.

Makes 9 servings

Nutrition information per serving:

Calories	105	Total Fat	0 g	Sodium	268 mg
Cholesterol	6 mg	Saturated Fat	0 g	Dietary Fiber	0 g

CHEWY LEMON–HONEY COOKIES

Prep Time: 20 minutes   Cook Time: 8 minutes

2 cups all-purpose flour
1½ teaspoons baking soda
½ cup honey
⅓ cup Fleischmann's Margarine,
    softened

¼ cup granulated sugar
1 tablespoon grated lemon peel
¼ cup EGG BEATERS
    Lemon Glaze, optional
    (page 81)

In small bowl, combine flour and baking soda; set aside.

In large bowl, with electric mixer at medium speed, beat honey, margarine, granulated sugar and lemon peel until creamy. Add Egg Beaters; beat until smooth. Gradually stir in flour mixture until blended.

Drop dough by rounded teaspoonfuls, 2 inches apart, onto lightly greased baking sheets. Bake at 350°F for 7 to 8 minutes or until lightly browned. Remove from sheets; cool completely on wire racks. Drizzle with Lemon Glaze if desired. *Makes 3½ dozen cookies*

LEMON GLAZE: In small bowl, combine 1 cup powdered sugar and 2 tablespoons lemon juice until smooth.

Nutrition information per serving:					
(1 cookie without glaze)					
Calories	52	Total Fat	1 g	Sodium	61 mg
Cholesterol	0 mg	Saturated Fat	0 g	Dietary Fiber	0 g

LEMON BARS

Prep Time: 25 minutes   Cook Time: 30 minutes

1¼ cups all-purpose flour, divided
 1 cup granulated sugar, divided
 ⅓ cup Fleischmann's Margarine,
  softened

½ cup EGG BEATERS
 2 teaspoons grated lemon peel
 ¼ cup lemon juice
  Powdered sugar, optional

In medium bowl, combine 1 cup flour and ¼ cup granulated sugar; cut in margarine until mixture resembles coarse crumbs. Press mixture onto bottom of 9-inch square baking pan. Bake at 350°F for 15 minutes or until lightly browned.

In small bowl, combine Egg Beaters, lemon peel, lemon juice, remaining flour and remaining granulated sugar; pour over prepared crust. Bake for 15 minutes more or until set. Cool slightly; sprinkle with powdered sugar if desired. Cool completely in pan on wire rack; cut into 32 (2×1-inch) bars.
Makes 32 bars

Nutrition information per serving:					
(1 bar without powdered sugar)					
Calories	60	Total Fat	2 g	Sodium	21 mg
Cholesterol	0 mg	Saturated Fat	0 g	Dietary Fiber	0 g

LIGHT & LUSCIOUS CHOCOLATE CAKE
WITH RASPBERRY SAUCE

Prep Time: 20 minutes   Cook Time: 35 minutes

2 cups all-purpose flour
1⅓ cups skim milk
1 cup sugar
1 cup EGG BEATERS
⅔ cup unsweetened cocoa
⅔ cup Fleischmann's Margarine, softened

1½ teaspoons baking powder
1½ teaspoons vanilla extract
½ teaspoon baking soda
Raspberry Sauce (recipe follows)
Fresh raspberries and fresh mint sprigs, for garnish

In large bowl, with electric mixer at medium speed, combine flour, milk, sugar, Egg Beaters, cocoa, margarine, baking powder, vanilla and baking soda just until blended. Beat at high speed for 3 minutes. Spread batter into lightly greased 13×9×2-inch baking pan. Bake at 350°F for 30 to 35 minutes or until toothpick inserted in center comes out clean. Cool in pan on wire rack. Cut into 16 (3×2-inch) pieces. Serve topped with Raspberry Sauce. Garnish with raspberries and mint.   *Makes 16 servings*

RASPBERRY SAUCE: In electric blender container, purée 2 cups thawed frozen raspberries in syrup; strain. Stir in 2 tablespoons sugar and 1 tablespoon cornstarch. In small saucepan, cook raspberry mixture until thickened and boiling. Cover; chill.

Nutrition information per serving:

(1 piece of cake, 2 tablespoons sauce)

Calories	238	Total Fat	8 g	Sodium	161 mg
Cholesterol	0 mg	Saturated Fat	2 g	Dietary Fiber	1 g

Light & Luscious Chocolate Cake
with Raspberry Sauce

CHOCOLATE ALMOND BISCOTTI

Prep Time: 25 minutes   Cook Time: 45 minutes

3 cups all-purpose flour
½ cup unsweetened cocoa
2 teaspoons baking powder
½ teaspoon salt
1 cup granulated sugar
⅔ cup Fleischmann's Margarine,
    softened

¾ cup EGG BEATERS
1 teaspoon almond extract
½ cup whole blanched almonds,
    toasted and coarsely
    chopped
Powdered Sugar Glaze (recipe
    follows)

In medium bowl, combine flour, cocoa, baking powder and salt; set aside.

In large bowl, with electric mixer at medium speed, beat granulated sugar
and margarine for 2 minutes or until creamy. Add Egg Beaters and almond
extract; beat well. With electric mixer at low speed, gradually add flour
mixture, beating just until blended; stir in almonds.

On lightly greased baking sheet, form dough into two (12×2½-inch) logs.
Bake at 350°F for 25 to 30 minutes or until toothpick inserted in centers
comes out clean. Remove from sheet; cool on wire racks 15 minutes.

Using serrated knife, slice each log diagonally into 12 (1-inch-thick) slices;
place, cut-sides up, on same baking sheet. Bake at 350°F for 12
to 15 minutes on each side or until cookies are crisp and edges are
browned. Remove from sheet; cool completely on wire rack. Drizzle tops
with Powdered Sugar Glaze.   *Makes 2 dozen cookies*

POWDERED SUGAR GLAZE: In small bowl, combine 1 cup
powdered sugar and 5 to 6 teaspoons water until smooth.

Nutrition Information per serving:

(1 biscotti)

Calories	160	Total Fat	7 g	Sodium	125 mg
Cholesterol	0 mg	Saturated Fat	1 g	Dietary Fiber	0 g

Chocolate Almond Biscotti

MOCHA MARBLE POUND CAKE

Prep Time: 20 minutes   Cook Time: 65 minutes

2 cups all-purpose flour
2 teaspoons baking powder
1 teaspoon baking soda
½ teaspoon salt
1 cup sugar
¼ cup Fleischmann's Margarine, softened

1 teaspoon vanilla extract
½ cup EGG BEATERS
1 (8-ounce) container low fat coffee yogurt
¼ cup unsweetened cocoa
Mocha Yogurt Glaze (recipe follows)

In small bowl, combine flour, baking powder, baking soda and salt; set aside.

In large bowl, with electric mixer at medium speed, beat sugar, margarine and vanilla until creamy. Add Egg Beaters; beat until smooth. With mixer at low speed, add yogurt alternately with flour mixture, beating well after each addition. Remove half of batter to medium bowl. Add cocoa to batter remaining in large bowl; beat until blended. Alternately spoon coffee and chocolate batters into greased 9×5×3-inch loaf pan. With knife, cut through batters to create marbled effect.

Bake at 325°F for 60 to 65 minutes or until toothpick inserted in center comes out clean. Cool in pan on wire rack for 10 minutes. Remove from pan; cool completely on wire rack. Frost with Mocha Yogurt Glaze.

Makes 16 servings

MOCHA YOGURT GLAZE: In small bowl, combine ½ cup powdered sugar, 1 tablespoon unsweetened cocoa and 1 tablespoon low fat coffee yogurt until smooth; add more yogurt if necessary to make spreading consistency.

Nutrition information per serving:					
Calories	159	Total Fat	3 g	Sodium	215 mg
Cholesterol	1 mg	Saturated Fat	1 g	Dietary Fiber	1 g

Mocha Marble Pound Cake

BLUEBERRY BREAD PUDDING WITH CARAMEL SAUCE

Prep Time: 20 minutes   **Cook Time: 1 hour**

8 slices white bread, cubed
1 cup fresh or frozen blueberries
2 cups skim milk
1 cup EGG BEATERS

⅔ cup sugar
1 teaspoon vanilla extract
¼ teaspoon ground cinnamon
   Caramel Sauce (recipe follows)

Place bread cubes in bottom of lightly greased 8×8×2-inch baking pan. Sprinkle with blueberries; set aside.

In large bowl, combine milk, Egg Beaters, sugar, vanilla and cinnamon; pour over bread mixture. Set pan in larger pan filled with 1-inch depth hot water. Bake at 350°F for 1 hour or until knife inserted in center comes out clean. Serve warm with Caramel Sauce.   *Makes 9 servings*

CARAMEL SAUCE: In small saucepan, over low heat, heat ¼ cup skim milk and 14 vanilla caramels until caramels are melted, stirring frequently.

Nutrition information per serving:

Calories	210	Total Fat	2 g	Sodium	227 mg
Cholesterol	2 mg	Saturated Fat	1 g	Dietary Fiber	1 g

FESTIVE EGG NOG

Prep Time: 15 minutes   **Cook Time: 25 minutes**

6 cups skim milk, divided
1 cup EGG BEATERS
½ cup sugar
1 teaspoon vanilla extract

1 teaspoon rum extract
¼ cup brandy, optional
   Ground nutmeg and
      cinnamon, for garnish

In large saucepan, over medium heat, heat 5 cups milk, Egg Beaters and sugar until thickened, stirring constantly. Remove from heat; stir in vanilla and rum extracts. Cover; chill at least 3 hours.

Just before serving, stir in brandy if desired; thin to desired consistency with remaining milk. Garnish with sprinkle of nutmeg and cinnamon.

Makes 8 servings

Nutrition information per serving:

(without brandy)

Calories	128	Total Fat	0 g	Sodium	133 mg
Cholesterol	4 mg	Saturated Fat	0 g	Dietary Fiber	0 g

Blueberry Bread Pudding with Caramel Sauce

MOCHA MARBLED CHEESECAKE

Prep Time: 30 minutes   Cook Time: 1 hour

1½ cups graham cracker crumbs
1 cup sugar, divided
¼ cup Fleischmann's Margarine, melted
1 (24-ounce) container low fat cottage cheese (1% milkfat)
2 cups EGG BEATERS, divided
2 (8-ounce) packages light cream cheese (Neufchâtel), softened

1 tablespoon unsweetened cocoa
1 teaspoon instant coffee powder
Light nondairy whipped topping, optional

In medium bowl, combine graham cracker crumbs, ¼ cup sugar and margarine. Press onto bottom and 2 inches up side of 9-inch springform pan; set aside.

In electric blender container or food processor, blend cottage cheese and ½ cup Egg Beaters until smooth, scraping down sides of container as necessary. In large bowl, with electric mixer at high speed, beat cream cheese, remaining sugar, cottage cheese mixture and remaining Egg Beaters until smooth. Remove ¾ cup mixture to small bowl; stir in cocoa and coffee powder. Alternately spoon vanilla and mocha batters into prepared crust. With knife, cut through batters to create marbled effect.

Bake at 325°F for 1 hour or until puffed and set. Cool in pan on wire rack 15 minutes. Carefully run metal spatula around edge of cheesecake to loosen. Cover; chill at least 3 hours. Top with whipped topping if desired.

Makes 16 servings

Nutrition information per serving:

(without topping)

Calories	219	Total Fat	9 g	Sodium	460 mg
Cholesterol	17 mg	Saturated Fat	4 g	Dietary Fiber	0 g

FAT–FREE CAPPUCCINO FLAN

Prep Time: 20 minutes   Cook Time: 40 minutes

1 cup EGG BEATERS
½ cup sugar
1 tablespoon instant espresso or
    coffee powder
½ teaspoon vanilla extract
⅛ teaspoon ground cinnamon

2⅓ cups skim milk, scalded and
    cooled 10 minutes
Light nondairy whipped
    topping and cocoa powder
    or additional ground
    cinnamon, optional

In medium bowl, combine Egg Beaters, sugar, espresso or coffee powder, vanilla and cinnamon. Gradually stir in milk. Pour into 6 lightly greased (6-ounce) custard cups or ramekins. Set cups in pan filled with 1-inch depth hot water.

Bake at 350°F for 35 to 40 minutes or until knife inserted in centers comes out clean. Remove cups from pan; cool to room temperature. Chill until firm, about 2 hours. To serve, loosen edges with knife; invert onto individual plates. Top with whipped topping and cocoa or cinnamon if desired.   *Makes 6 servings*

Nutrition information per serving:

(without topping)

Calories	120	Total Fat	0 g	Sodium	116 mg
Cholesterol	2 mg	Saturated Fat	0 g	Dietary Fiber	0 g

FAT–FREE TROPICAL SHAKE

Prep Time: 5 minutes

1 cup EGG BEATERS
1 cup cold skim milk
1 small banana, cut into chunks

1 small mango,* peeled and cut
    into chunks (about 1 cup)

In electric blender container, blend Egg Beaters, milk, banana and mango for 1 minute or until smooth. Serve immediately.

Makes 4 (8-ounce) servings

*One cup guava, papaya or pineapple chunks may be substituted.

Note: Refrigerate unused portion. Must be used within 48 hours.

Nutrition information per serving:

Calories	98	Total Fat	0 g	Sodium	133 mg
Cholesterol	1 mg	Saturated Fat	0 g	Dietary Fiber	1 g

Index